Dolphins

Dolphins

by Sally M. Walker

A Carolrhoda Nature Watch Book

Carolrhoda Books, Inc. / Minneapolis

*For my sister Donna MacArt Havrisko,
who also rode Mitzi, and Aisling Power,
my Irish "daughter" who collects dolphins*

*The publisher would like to thank Robyn P. Angliss, fishery
biologist, National Marine Fisheries Service; Wanda L. Cain,
fishery biologist, National Marine Fisheries Service; and Kyler
Abernathy, biologist, University of Minnesota, for their
assistance with this book.*

Carolrhoda Books, Inc., c/o The Lerner Publishing Group
241 First Avenue North, Minneapolis, MN 55401 U.S.A.

Website address: www.lernerbooks.com

LIBRARY OF CONGRESS CATALOGING-IN-PUBLICATION DATA

Walker, Sally M.
    Dolphins / by Sally M. Walker.
        p.   cm.
    "A Carolrhoda nature watch book."
    Includes index.
    Summary: Introduces these aquatic mammals by de-
scribing their physical characteristics, life cycle, behavior,
relations with humans, and threats to their survival.
    ISBN 1–57505–221–0 (alk. paper)
    1. Dolphins—Juvenile literature. [1. Dolphins.] I. Title.
QL737.C432W35 1999
599.53—dc21   98-3503

Manufactured in the United States of America
1 2 3 4 5 6 – JR – 04 03 02 01 00 99

CONTENTS

WHAT IS A DOLPHIN?

Imagine yourself swimming through the salty water of an ocean bay. Just beneath the water's surface, a dark shape glides swiftly toward you. A gray fin pokes above the water. Something like this happened to me when I was 11 years old. But I wasn't scared. Although I would never touch a dolphin in the wild, my family was visiting a dolphin research facility, and my sister and I were allowed to swim with a bottlenose dolphin. The dolphin's trainer had explained just what to do. I held onto the fin on the dolphin's back, and she pulled me through the water. What I remember most about the ride were the up-and-down motions of the dolphin's tail and realizing how powerful her muscles were. Although my ride lasted only a few minutes, it was long enough to trigger a lifelong love of dolphins.

Dolphins are **aquatic** animals, which means they live in the water. But dolphins are not fish—they are mammals, animals that produce milk for their babies' nourishment. Dolphins, porpoises, and certain kinds of whales make up a group of mammals called the Odontoceti (oh-dahnt-uh-SEE-ty). The Odontoceti have large heads, hairless bodies, paddle-shaped front limbs, and teeth. The name comes from two Greek words, *odontos* and *ketos*, meaning "toothed whale."

7

Biologists, or people who study living things, divide the Odontoceti into several smaller groups called families. Three of the families are marine dolphins, river dolphins, and porpoises. *Marine* means belonging to the sea. Marine dolphins live in all the world's oceans and make up the family Delphinidae (del-FIN-uh-dee). Within the family are even smaller groups called species. There are 32 species of marine dolphins. Pilot whales and killer whales are two species of the marine dolphin family, even though they are called whales.

River dolphins live in freshwater, or water that is not salty like the ocean. They make up the family Platanistidae (pla-ta-NIS-tih-dee). There are six species of river dolphins found in several river systems in South America, India, and China.

Porpoises are known as the family Phocoenidae (foh-SEE-nuh-dee). People often use the names *dolphin* and *porpoise* interchangeably, but dolphins and porpoises are different animals. This book discusses members of the marine and river dolphin families.

Among the 32 species of marine dolphins are spinner (above), common, spotted, dusky, bottlenose, Pacific white-sided, and Atlantic white-sided dolphins, as well as pilot whales (right) and killer whales.

8

River dolphins include the La Plata, whitefin, two species of Ganges (one shown above), and two species of Amazon dolphins. A porpoise (right) is a different animal than a dolphin.

Forty-five to fifty million years ago, warm seas covered more of the earth's surface than they do now. The ancient ancestors of **cetaceans** (sih-TAY-shuns), a group of marine mammals made up of all whales, porpoises, and dolphins, were four-legged mammals who lived on land. Perhaps because they could find plenty of food in the widespread sea, the cetacean ancestors began spending most of their time in the water.

Over millions of years, the bodies of these mammals changed in many ways to **adapt,** or become better suited, to living in the water. Front legs **evolved,** or gradually changed, into paddle-shaped **pectoral fins,** or flippers. Hind legs disappeared completely. To make it easier to breathe with much of the body underwater, nostrils shifted from the front of the face to the top of the head, where they became a single **blowhole.** Most descendants also developed a **dorsal fin,** or a fin on their back.

Throughout millions of years, different species of dolphins, whales, and porpoises evolved from these ancient ancestors. None of the ancient species have survived. The earliest known **fossils,** or bones that have hardened and turned to stone, of the family Delphinidae are about 11 million years old.

The long snout and "grin" of a bottlenose dolphin are appealing to many people.

Some dolphins, like this Pacific white-sided dolphin, have a shorter, rounded snout.

PHYSICAL CHARACTERISTICS

When you think of dolphins, the first picture that pops into your head may be the familiar long snout and toothy "grin" of a bottlenose dolphin. Bottlenose dolphins are the species most commonly seen in zoos, in movies, and on television. Perhaps people enjoy them because their smiles make them look happy. But dolphins do not control their smiley appearance—the position of their bones and muscles results in that expression.

Many other dolphin species, including spinner, common, and spotted dolphins, have long snouts like the bottlenose. Some species—killer whales, Commerson's dolphins, and Risso's dolphins—have very short snouts or none at all, like porpoises. No matter what the length of their snout, all dolphin species have bodies that are wonderfully adapted to living in the water.

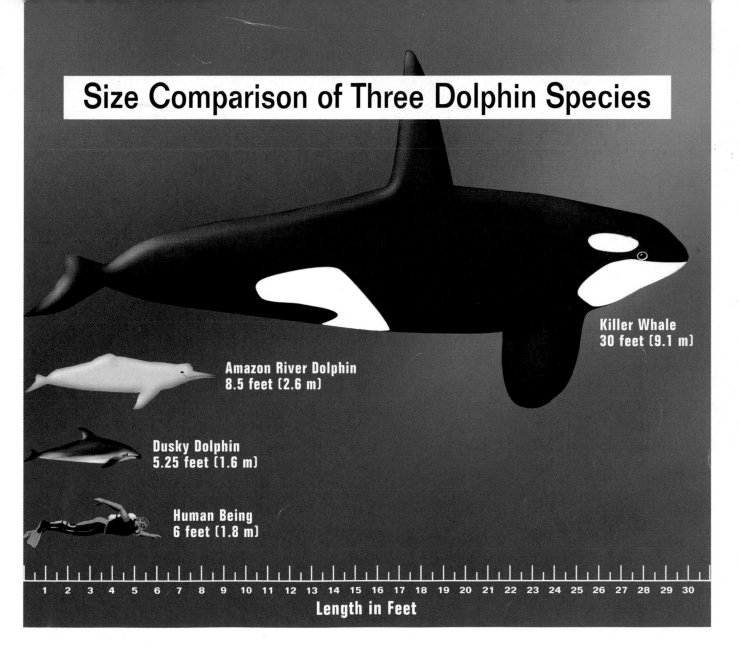

Size Comparison of Three Dolphin Species

Killer Whale
30 feet (9.1 m)

Amazon River Dolphin
8.5 feet (2.6 m)

Dusky Dolphin
5.25 feet (1.6 m)

Human Being
6 feet (1.8 m)

1 2 3 4 5 6 7 8 9 10 11 12 13 14 15 16 17 18 19 20 21 22 23 24 25 26 27 28 29 30

Length in Feet

The length and weight of a dolphin's body vary greatly among species, from about the size of a human to about five times that length. In general, males are larger than females. Dusky dolphins grow to about 5 feet 3 inches long (1.6 m) and weigh at least 265 pounds (120 kg).

Amazon river dolphins grow to be up to 8 feet 6 inches long (2.6 m) and can weigh up to 350 pounds (160 kg). Male killer whales may reach 31 feet long (9.5 m) and weigh up to 8.8 tons (8 metric tons). Female killer whales may reach 23 feet long (7 m) and weigh up to 4.4 tons (4 metric tons).

11

A leaping bottlenose dolphin displays its torpedo shape, front flippers, curved dorsal fin, and flukes.

A dolphin's torpedo shape helps it move swiftly and smoothly through the water. Dolphins cruise at speeds averaging 3 to 4 miles per hour (5–6 km/h), although researchers have observed some dolphins traveling an average of 6 to 9 miles per hour (10–15 km/h). Spotted dolphins are one of the fastest dolphin species. They have been timed for short sprints at speeds close to 25 miles per hour (40 km/h).

Powerful tail fins, called **flukes,** drive a dolphin's body forward. A dolphin's flukes move up and down, unlike a fish's tail, which moves from side to side. A dolphin's tail muscles are strong enough to enable it to jump high out of the water. In fact, dolphins performing in shows are able to take fish from trainers standing on platforms 15 feet (4.6 m) above the water.

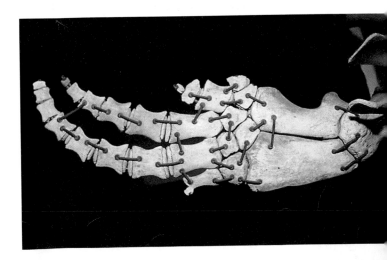

Above: *A killer whale's triangular dorsal fin*
Top right: *A Commerson's dolphin's rounded dorsal fin*
Middle right: *An Amazon river dolphin's tiny dorsal fin*
Bottom right: *The bones of a flipper*

Most dolphins have a dorsal fin that keeps them upright and prevents their bodies from spinning while they swim. Dorsal fins vary in shape. Atlantic white-sided, Pacific white-sided, bottlenose, and spotted dolphins have a sickle-shaped, or curved, fin. Commerson's dolphins have a rounded dorsal fin. Spinner dolphins and adult male killer whales have a very triangular dorsal fin. Amazon river dolphins have practically no dorsal fin at all.

Two front flippers help steady the dolphin and are also used for steering. The skeleton inside the front flippers contains five bony "fingers," which are last remnants of the ancient ancestor's legs. Tail flukes and dorsal fins are made of thick tissue and are boneless.

Above: *Spotted dolphins are heavily spotted as adults but don't have any spots when they are young.*
Left: *A dolphin's skin is often covered with scars from encounters with other dolphins or from attacks by enemies such as sharks.*

Most mammals have hairy skin—but dolphins don't. Marine dolphins have smooth skin that feels like a warm, wet rubber ball. An Amazon river dolphin's skin feels more like a soft, wet leather glove. Amazon river dolphins sometimes have a few bristles on their snouts; otherwise, they are hairless.

A dolphin's skin is easily injured and is very sensitive to sunlight. When researchers capture a dolphin, they take great care to keep its skin moist and protected from sunburn.

Dolphins' skin color varies according to species. Most species are various shades of black, white, and gray. The color patterns are often very beautiful. Many people recognize the stunning black and white of a killer whale. Atlantic white-sided dolphins are black and white with a band of gray and a patch of yellow or tan. Newborn spotted dolphins have gray backs and ivory-colored bellies, but adults have heavily spotted bodies and black masks.

Left: *The black and white of a killer whale is easily recognizable.*
Below: *A dolphin's blowhole curves toward the dolphin's back.*

A layer of blubber about an inch thick lies under a dolphin's skin. Like all mammals, dolphins maintain a regular body temperature, which is 97–99°F (36–37°C). That is about the same as ours. The blubber is important for keeping a dolphin warm in cold waters. The thick blubber layer also makes it difficult for a shark's teeth to slice deeply into a dolphin's body.

A dolphin breathes through the blowhole on top of its head. Most blowholes are crescent shaped and curve toward the dolphin's back. The blowhole is normally closed, but it opens when a dolphin surfaces to take a breath. When the dolphin exhales, the hole opens again and a puff or popping sound is made when the old air rushes out. Sometimes there is a tiny cloud of mist—but not a plume like there is when a whale exhales.

A dolphin's trachea, or windpipe, is a separate tube from its esophagus, the tube that carries food to the stomach. This allows dolphins to breathe and swallow food at the same time. The human trachea and esophagus are not completely separate—that's why we can choke if we talk or breathe while we are swallowing food.

Dolphins such as these two spinner dolphins can dive deeper and stay underwater a lot longer than humans.

Dolphins can remain underwater much longer than we can. Some species can remain under for 7 minutes or longer. That's because their bodies use oxygen, the gas we breathe from the air, differently than we do. Dolphins' bodies use more oxygen from each breath than our bodies do. This allows them to go a lot longer between breaths than we can. They also need fewer breaths per minute. An adult human male takes about 16 breaths per minute. A dolphin about the same size needs only 1 to 3 breaths per minute.

Dolphins can also dive deeper than we can. When we are underwater, the water above us pushes against our bodies. If we go too deep, our bodies will be squeezed tightly enough to crack our rigid rib cages. Divers can feel the squeeze at 100 to 130 feet (30.5–39.6 m). To go deeper is risking injury or death. Unlike our ribs, a dolphin's ribs are flexible, or able to bend. When a dolphin swims into deep water, its ribs do not break; they fold inward. Its lungs also collapse. As a dolphin surfaces, its ribs and lungs resume their normal positions. During the 1960s, a bottlenose dolphin named Tuffy worked with the United States Navy. He was trained to push a camera button and take his own picture. From a depth of 984 feet (300 m), Tuffy's picture clearly showed his squeezed-in sides where his lungs and ribs had collapsed.

Dolphins have sharp, cone-shaped teeth. This shape is perfect for grasping **prey,** or animals that are killed for food. The shape of their teeth is one way to tell the difference between dolphins and porpoises. Porpoises have flattened, shovel-like teeth, something like the teeth next to your two front top teeth.

Almost all mammals produce baby, or milk, teeth. These fall out and are replaced by adult teeth that the animal uses for the rest of its life. Dolphins, however, produce only one set of teeth that remains in place throughout the dolphin's life.

A dolphin's teeth grow in layers, somewhat like the growth layers inside tree trunks. New layers form on the inside of the tooth. By counting the patterns of layers, researchers can determine how old the dolphin is.

Dolphins in captivity often show preferences for certain kinds of fish, so they seem to have a sense of taste. During the 1980s, researchers conducted taste tests on a bottlenose dolphin to see if it could tell the difference between pure water and liquids that tasted bitter, salty, sweet, or sour. The dolphin could distinguish between the water and the other liquids. Unlike humans, however, dolphins have little or no sense of smell.

All dolphins have sharp, cone-shaped teeth, although most dolphins' teeth aren't as big as a killer whale's.

Marine dolphins have large eyes on the sides of their heads. They can see well in and out of the water.

A marine dolphin's eyes are on the sides of its head. Marine dolphins see well in and out of the water. Dolphins in captivity have no difficulty leaping into the air and removing pieces of fish from a trainer's hand. River dolphins, on the other hand, have poor eyesight, and their eyes are noticeably smaller than a marine dolphin's eyes. Ganges river dolphins have very tiny eyes that can detect light, but they are essentially blind. The water where these dolphins live is muddy and murky. Their small eyes and poor eyesight evolved over many thousands of years in the dim light. Like many creatures who live in dark places, river dolphins rely on other senses, particularly hearing, for information.

In fact, all dolphin species rely on good hearing. Dolphins do not have an external (outside the body) ear. They have pinhole openings on each side of the head. But a dolphin's jawbone and the fatty tissue surrounding it are much more important for hearing. They carry sound waves directly to the dolphin's middle and inner ear, where sound is sensed. Dolphins can hear sounds that are much too high-pitched for human ears to hear.

River dolphins, such as this Amazon river dolphin, have tiny eyes and poor eyesight. Although they have no visible ears, dolphins rely heavily on their hearing.

COMMUNICATION AND ECHOLOCATION

Dolphins make sounds that biologists place into two broad groups: **whistles** and **clicks.** Whistles include squawks, squeals, and squeaky noises. They are usually lower pitched than clicks and are within the range of sound that humans can hear. Whistles are made by blowing air through the nasal system, or passages of the nose. They seem to be one way dolphins communicate with each other. Whistles can last less than a second, but might last up to 3 seconds or longer. Whistles are louder from an open blowhole.

One type of whistle is a **signature whistle.** This is a specific whistle that a dolphin uses to identify itself, much like you use your name to set you apart from other people. Do other dolphins associate a specific signature whistle with a specific dolphin? Biologists think they do. Some test results indicate that dolphins imitate the signature whistles of other dolphins they live with. This may be a way of calling to a specific individual and getting it to call back in response, so each can find the other.

These two spotted dolphins might use sounds called whistles in order to communicate with each other.

In echolocation, sound waves are sent out from a dolphin's head. When the sound waves hit an object, they return to the dolphin as an echo. This enables the dolphin to detect the object.

Clicks are very high-pitched sounds that humans cannot hear. Researchers are not sure how dolphins make clicks. Some believe clicks are produced in the larynx, or vocal cords, the way humans make sound. However, more researchers believe clicks are made when air passing through a dolphin's nasal system causes flaps of skin to vibrate.

Dolphins use clicks in their **echolocation** system. In echolocation, a dolphin strings clicks together in bursts of sound called **click trains.** Click trains form sound waves that leave a dolphin's head and spread through the water similar to the way a flashlight's beam spreads in

the dark. When click train sound waves hit an object, they bounce off the object's surface and race back toward the dolphin—the way your voice echoes back to you in a big, empty room.

Dolphins can make click train bursts that contain more than 700 clicks per second. They can tell an object's size, shape, and distance by listening to the differences in click echoes. How often a dolphin sends clicks and how rapidly it strings them together depend on how far away an object is, how big the object is, and how interested the dolphin is in locating it. Distant, small, and interesting objects are sent frequent and rapid clicks.

You may have noticed that a dolphin has a large forehead. The lumpy appearance is caused by an organ called the **melon,** which plays an important role in echolocation. The melon is about the size and shape of the small fruit with the same name. It is made of oily tissue that is a good carrier of sound. The melon helps direct sound waves as they are sent from the dolphin's head.

Biologists measure clicks with underwater-listening devices called **hydrophones.** By listening in on the dolphin's echolocation system, scientists hope to discover how dolphins can distinguish so well between distant objects that are close to the same size. Scientific studies have shown that a dolphin can locate an object about the size of a tangerine more than 330 feet away (100 m)— a distance longer than a football field.

A dolphin's large forehead is due to the melon, an organ that aids in echolocation.

LIFE CYCLE

Most dolphin species live for 15 years; some species live for 25 years. Pilot whales may live 50 years, and female killer whales may live to be 80.

Female dolphins are ready to have their first **calf,** or baby, when they are 8 to 12 years old. Since newborn calves do not have a thick blubber layer to keep them warm, mating is timed so that most calves are born during warm months. After mating, the male and female do not remain together.

Gestation, or the time in which a calf grows inside its mother, varies among dolphin species. The average time is 10 to 12 months. Killer whales and pilot whales have gestation periods of about 16 months.

Calves are born underwater, usually tail first. A newborn calf is about half the length of its mother and about one-sixth her weight. Bottlenose calves are about 3.5 to 4 feet long (1.0–1.2 m) and weigh around 30 pounds (13.6 kg). Unless they are sickly, newborn calves are good swimmers and they travel close to their mothers, usually alongside her dorsal fin.

Within an hour of birth, a calf will nurse from its mother. A dolphin calf cannot suck on its mother's nipple because the calf's hard, bony snout does not have flexible lips. Instead, the calf wraps its tongue around the nipple and milk squirts into the calf's mouth. A calf nurses about every 20 minutes. A mother dolphin's milk is almost half fat (cow's milk is only about 4 percent fat), so a calf grows quickly. Its weight will double by the time it is 2 months old.

A newborn bottlenose calf swims alongside its mother's dorsal fin.

Mother dolphins form strong bonds with their calves. Groups of mothers and calves are the largest of the dolphin social groups.

At about 6 months of age, a calf starts eating fish. In addition to eating solid food, calves nurse for 16 months to 2 or 3 years. Biologists have even observed a 4-year-old calf nursing.

The bond between a mother dolphin and her calf is the strongest of all dolphin relationships. Depending on the species, calves may remain with their mothers for 3 to 6 years, or even for life. One bottlenose mother and calf, observed for many years as part of a research project, were still together 10 years after the calf was born. Groups made up of mothers and calves are the largest of several kinds of dolphin social groups.

When calves leave their mothers, they join small groups of other **subadults,** dolphins who are not fully grown. Subadult groups may include male and female members, or they may have members of just one sex. Young dolphins belong to these groups for several years.

Subadult females tend to associate with adults more than subadult males do. They also join an adult group (usually a mother-calf group) at an earlier age—when they are between 8 and 12 years old. This may be because they are old enough to bear a calf. Some females return to the group they belonged to when they were born.

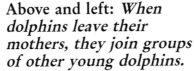

Above and left: *When dolphins leave their mothers, they join groups of other young dolphins.*

Males remain in subadult groups (often all male) until they are 10 to 15 years old. By that age, they associate less and less with younger subadults. They form young adult groups—usually two or three individuals of the same age. They are extremely effective in swimming, hunting, and probably communicating as a unit. The bonds between the males are long lasting and may even be lifelong. Biologists do not know why young male dolphins form these closely bonded groups, but it may be for protection. This would be especially important if animals that hunt dolphins, such as sharks or killer whales, were around. It is also possible that males form these bonds because they are related to each other. Further research will help determine if this is true.

SCHOOLS AND DAILY ROUTINE

The small social groups of marine dolphins make up a larger group called a **school.** A school's size depends on species and on the location of the **home range,** or area where the group lives. A large home range may include 500 or more square miles (1,295 sq km). Such a range in deep, open water most likely offers a large quantity of food and can support a large dolphin population. Small home ranges in shallow water or sheltered areas, such as small harbors and bays, often have less food and can support fewer dolphins. Schools of common or spotted dolphins in the open sea often have more than 1,000 members. Schools of bottlenose dolphins, especially those in shallow water, may have less than 20 members.

A school of dolphins in the open sea, such as this school of common dolphins, can contain more than 1,000 members.

This school of spinner dolphins is made up of several smaller groups.

For almost 20 years, Dr. Randall Wells has been studying a community of about one hundred wild bottlenose dolphins that live in Sarasota Bay in Florida. His research indicates that the number of dolphins in a school stays pretty much the same from year to year, although some individuals move in and out. Calves tend to remain in the school's home range until they are almost grown up. When they are mature, they might join a new school. Groups of adult males sometimes swim away from the community and mate with females from other schools. They may be gone from their home range for months or even years.

Hunting is an important part of a dolphin's daily routine. Different species of dolphins hunt different prey. Pilot whales and Risso's dolphins eat squid, octopus, and cuttlefish. Spinner and common dolphins prefer fish. Killer whales will eat fish, and some will hunt seals and other dolphins. Bottlenose dolphins feed mostly on fish and shrimp. River dolphins eat snails, eels, and sometimes crabs. An adult dolphin will eat about 10 to 20 pounds (4.5–9.0 kg) of food per day, depending on the dolphin's size and species.

Dolphin hunting patterns depend on the prey. If hunting a single fish, a dolphin will likely chase it and gulp it down. If the prey live in schools (the way squid and the fish anchovy and mullet do), dolphins may work together to catch them. Small groups of dolphins, or sometimes individuals, separate from the school and scout, or look, for food. Biologists believe the scouts relay information about the prey and their location back to the main school of dolphins. When the group finds a school of fish, the dolphins move in patterns that make the hunt more successful.

Sometimes an entire school of dolphins hunts together. This school of common dolphins is herding fish in the Sea of Cortez in Mexico.

Right: *A school of fish provides an easy meal for a dusky dolphin.*
Bottom right: *Killer whales sometimes approach shore to attack sea lions.*

If there is a large number of prey, and the whole dolphin school is participating in the chase, the dolphins circle the prey, slowly making their circle smaller. This packs the prey tightly together so they are easier to catch. Dolphins often swim under the prey as well, which packs them even more tightly.

A hunting group might also drive a school of fish toward shore or toward a wall of waiting dolphins. Like the circling pattern, the shore or dolphin wall acts as a barrier that prevents the prey's escape.

These common dolphins are porpoising—a rapid and graceful way for dolphins to glide through the water.

When chasing prey, dolphins typically move by **porpoising,** a type of fairly rapid swimming combined with jumps of 12 to 20 inches (30.5–50.8 cm) out of the water. Porpoising dolphins reenter the water without making a splash. Dolphins may also **breach,** or jump partway out of the water and land on their side with a large splash. Since breaching is usually done while hunting, the splash is probably intended to drive prey in a specific direction.

You might think it would be difficult for dolphins to sleep in the water, but they sleep about a third of the day. One side of a dolphin's brain sleeps while the other remains awake. The part of the brain that stays awake sends messages to the dolphin's respiratory, or breathing, system so the dolphin surfaces for air every few minutes. If this didn't happen, the dolphin would drown.

By breaching, this dusky dolphin (top right) *and killer whale* (above) *are possibly trying to drive prey in a specific direction.*

When dolphins aren't hunting or resting, they spend time socializing, or mingling with other dolphins. Physical contact is an important part of the way they socialize. Dolphins often nudge each other with their snouts. They frequently brush bodies and stroke other members of their small group with their fins or tail flukes.

Dolphins, particularly calves and subadults, also seem to enjoy playing. Tailsplashing, twisting jumps, and chases are common forms of play. Among the subadults, the play sometimes gets rough, and tail slaps and biting occur. It is possible the roughhousing is a way of establishing who is the **dominant,** or highest ranking, dolphin.

Researchers have observed dolphins playing in captivity and in the wild. Some dolphins in oceanariums (marine aquariums) play with objects such as rings or balls even when no rewards or treats are given for the behavior. Dolphins in the wild play with potential prey such as jellyfish without actually eating them. Dolphins sometimes play by scooting backward along the surface of the water on their tails. Riding a boat's waves seems to be fun for dolphins, too, as well as a way to get a free ride.

Socializing is important for dolphins. A bottlenose dolphin gives a companion a friendly nudge (above), *and a small group of Pacific white-sided dolphins frolics together* (right).

The dolphins in Project Delphis, a research project at Sea Life Park Hawaii, enjoy blowing bubbles. In fact, they can blow bubble rings large enough to swim through! The dolphins at Sea Life Park Hawaii blow rings more than dolphins in other oceanariums. No one knows why. But biologists do know that blowing rings is not a trick done only by captive dolphins—they have seen wild Pacific spinner dolphins and Atlantic spotted dolphins do it, too. Blowing rings takes practice. Dolphins who are unable to do it can learn how by watching others and experimenting. The learning process must involve some type of thinking skills. Are dolphins really that smart?

Riding the waves of a ship is great fun for dolphins (top left), *as is walking backward on their tails* (above).

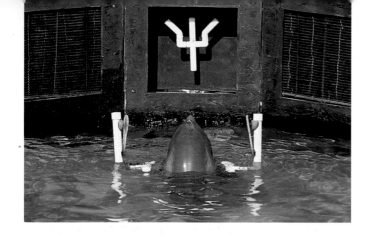

A dolphin intelligence test. A bottlenose dolphin is shown a sample pattern (top), the pattern disappears (middle), and the dolphin picks the matching pattern (bottom).

DOLPHINS AND INTELLIGENCE

Animals with high levels of intelligence tend to have brains with a lot of ridges and grooves on the surface. Skills such as thinking, memory, and speech are associated with this area of the brain. A dolphin's brain has a more folded surface than a human brain. Does this mean dolphins are smarter than people? Probably not. Even though a dolphin's brain has more folds, the layer of folded tissue in a human brain is almost twice as thick as the tissue in a dolphin's brain.

Dolphins are definitely good at learning. They understand gestures that ask for certain behaviors. For example, a trainer may use hand signals for "jump" and "hoop." Dolphins trained to understand the signals will jump through a hoop. Sounds such as whistles have also been used as signals. Some dolphins have learned to understand commands that tell them to find specific objects on the ocean floor.

Dolphins are very good at learning from a human trainer.

Researchers working with Project Delphis have conducted experiments to determine if dolphins recognize themselves as individuals. When you look in a mirror, you know the image you see is yourself, not another person. Some apes realize mirror images are reflections of themselves, but most animals do not. The researchers with Project Delphis painted marks on dolphins' bodies. When shown their reflections in a mirror, the dolphins twisted their bodies, trying to see the mark. You might do the same if a mark were painted on your body. The researchers believe the dolphins recognized themselves in the mirror. This behavior may be an indication of self-awareness and intelligence.

This dusky dolphin was caught in an illegal hunt in South America.

DOLPHINS AND PEOPLE

Since the times of the ancient Greeks, around 500 B.C., people have told stories about humans saved from drowning by dolphins who carried them to shore. Dolphins performing in oceanariums fascinate us, and sea travelers enjoy watching dolphins frolic alongside boats. People seem to feel a connection with dolphins, perhaps because they seem playful, or maybe because we think of them as gentle creatures. Whatever the reasons, dolphins are often referred to as "our friends in the sea." While this may be true, it is also true that people are a dolphin's enemies.

Killer whales and sharks prey on dolphins for food, but many more thousands of dolphins have been killed by human activity. Mass killings of hundreds of dolphins have occurred in Japan, Greenland, and parts of South America. The meat is used for food, fertilizer, and pet food. In some areas, the dolphin population has become sparse.

Hundreds of thousands of dolphins have been killed in the nets of fishers, people who catch fish to sell. **Purse seine (SAYN) nets** and **drift nets** are two kinds of fishing nets used by fishers. Purse seine nets are widely used in tuna fishing. They are long rectangular nets with floats attached to the top and a drawstring threaded through the bottom. Purse seine nets are set in a large circle. Fish are trapped when the net's drawstring is pulled tight. In the eastern tropical Pacific Ocean, schools of yellowfin tuna often travel near dolphins. One way to fish for tuna is to purposely encircle a school of dolphins with the purse seine net in order to catch the tuna swimming below. When fishers do this, dolphins may get trapped in the netting, too.

Drift nets are made of almost invisible netting with floats attached to it. In the past, a single net was often close to 4 miles long (6.4 km). Before laws were passed to limit drift nets, fishers would string 8 to 10 of them across wide areas of open sea. Drift nets are used to catch swordfish, sharks, and other fish, but any creature that runs into one can be caught. If dolphins are caught, they are unable to surface for air and they drown.

A purse seine fishing boat

This purse seiner is performing a backdown. Notice the dolphins at center that have escaped from the net.

During the 1960s and early 1970s, 200,000 to 300,000 dolphins per year were killed by fishers. In response to pressure from environmental groups and other concerned people who wanted to stop the killing of dolphins (as well as the killing of other marine mammals such as whales and baby harp seals), the United States passed the Marine Mammal Protection Act in 1972. This law made it illegal for U.S. fishers and companies to purposely harm dolphins (and other marine mammals), and limited the number of dolphins fishers were allowed to kill accidentally. Observers were placed on fishing ships to record how many dolphins the fishers killed. Dolphins could be captured for display or research only by people with special permission.

To reduce dolphin deaths, the U.S. government worked with the tuna fishing industry in the 1970s to develop a procedure called a **backdown,** which is used by purse seine fishers. During a backdown, fishers allow the far end of a purse seine net to dip below the water's surface enough to let dolphins swim away without releasing the yellowfin tuna.

In 1990, the United States made it illegal to buy yellowfin tuna from countries that allowed fishers to encircle dolphins. Fishers who wanted to sell tuna to companies in the United States had to use a different fishing method. Another method fishers could use besides encircling dolphins would be to encircle floating objects such as logs or large clumps of debris, hoping to find tuna grouped below. Fishers could also simply encircle schools of tuna.

Gradually, the countries that were banned from selling tuna in the United States have changed their fishing methods. It has made a difference. By 1993, the number of dolphins killed each year in the eastern tropical Pacific Ocean was less than five thousand, and by 1997, the number of dolphins killed dropped below three thousand.

In 1997, the ban was lifted on countries that were not allowed to sell their tuna in the United States. Fishers had to agree to kill no more than five thousand dolphins each year. Biologists believe that dolphin populations can recover and survive if yearly losses are held to this amount.

Purse seine fishing is not the only type of fishing that has been regulated. In 1993, the United Nations stopped the use of drift nets longer than about 2 miles (3.2 km) in international waters, or areas of the ocean that are outside the control of any nation. Drift nets that are up to 1.5 miles long (2.4 km) are still used in the United States to catch swordfish and sharks, and shorter nets are used to catch many species of fish. Some U.S. drift net fishers kill marine mammals, and the U.S. government is working with fishers, researchers, and environmental groups to develop new fishing methods that will reduce the number of marine mammals that are killed.

The dolphin-safe seal on a can of tuna informs consumers that no harm was done to dolphins in the capture of the tuna.

Dolphins becoming accidentally entangled in nets is still a problem. Some fishers and scientists have begun experimenting with warning alarms attached to nets. The alarms warn dolphins of the net so they can avoid it. This may be a successful way to prevent dolphins from being killed, but the procedure is still being tested.

Nets aren't the only dangers caused by people. Sometimes dolphins are injured by boat propellers. In nice weather, pleasure boats crowd the water of many bays, disturbing the dolphins' daily routine.

Pollution is another source of concern for the good health of dolphins. Chemicals are often dumped into water systems. This is of immediate concern for river dolphins, as rivers are often the site of chemical dumping. Some chemicals flow downriver into bays and oceans where they affect marine dolphins. Chemicals irritate a dolphin's skin and are absorbed through the skin into the dolphin's body. Chemicals can also become concentrated in the bodies of dolphins' prey. When a dolphin eats the prey, the chemicals are stored in the dolphin's blubber. The chemicals may not affect the dolphin's health immediately, but if the dolphin experiences a food shortage, its body draws on the blubber. Then the chemicals may harm the dolphin.

Waste dumped into rivers can make its way to the ocean, causing health problems for dolphins.

Development such as this along the Ganges River in India has reduced the habitat of the Ganges river dolphin.

Destruction of **habitat,** or the areas where dolphins normally live, is another problem. Overbuilding of homes, offices, and industrial plants along ocean coastlines and riverbanks destroys the habitat of many dolphins. Development like this has severely reduced the habitat of whitefin river dolphins in the Yangtze River in China. Dams on rivers where dolphins live reduce the dolphins' habitat by controlling or stopping the flow of the river. In South America, water for crops is drained from smaller rivers along the Amazon River. This has dried up many areas where the Amazon river dolphin once lived.

Long-term studies of wild and captive dolphins are helping us understand dolphin echolocation, life cycles, and schools. But the information gathered so far is only a start in reducing the threat to dolphins. Limits on the number of dolphins caught for food, fertilizer, and pet food may be necessary in the future. Fishers must continue to be responsible in their netting practices to ensure that they don't harm dolphins. Scientists and fishers will have to work together to seek solutions that will be acceptable to both groups.

As we increase our knowledge of dolphins and the role they play in the world's oceans, we can learn how to be more responsible in the way we treat the oceans and the animals who live there. If we do, then we can truthfully say we are good friends to dolphins.

GLOSSARY

adapt: to change in order to fit into one's environment

aquatic: living or occurring in water

backdown: a procedure in which one end of a purse seine net drops beneath the surface of the water so dolphins that are trapped can escape

blowhole: a nostril at the top of a dolphin's head

breach: to leap out of the water and land with a big splash

calf: a baby dolphin

cetaceans: a group of mammals made up of dolphins, porpoises, and whales

click trains: bursts of sound that dolphins make so they can locate objects by listening for echoes

clicks: high-pitched noises made by dolphins

dominant: the highest ranking or most powerful member of a group

dorsal fin: the fin on a dolphin's back

drift nets: long fishing nets that can be strung across miles of open sea

echolocation: finding an object by listening for echoes off its surface

evolve: to gradually change from one form to another

flukes: a dolphin's tail fins

fossils: plant or animal remains that have turned to stone

habitat: the type of environment in which an animal lives, such as an ocean or a river

home range: the geographical area where an animal lives

hydrophones: underwater-listening devices that researchers use to listen to dolphins

melon: a fatty organ in a dolphin's head that helps direct the sounds that dolphins use to locate objects

pectoral fins: the front flippers on a dolphin's sides

porpoising: rapid swimming combined with low jumps out of the water

prey: animals hunted by other animals for food

purse seine nets: large fishing nets commonly used to trap tuna

school: a group of dolphins that live, hunt, and interact with each other

signature whistle: a specific noise that a dolphin uses to identify itself

subadults: dolphins that are no longer calves but are not fully grown

whistles: noises made by dolphins, probably to communicate with each other

INDEX

ABOUT THE AUTHOR

Sally M. Walker is the author of numerous science books for children, including *Earthquakes, Rhinos, Hippos,* and *Sea Horses,* all published by Carolrhoda Books. Although her favorite job is writing, Ms. Walker also works as a children's literature consultant and has taught children's literature at Northern Illinois University. While she writes, Ms. Walker is usually surrounded by her family's golden retriever and two cats, who don't say very much but provide good company. She lives in Illinois with her husband and two children.